Lunch at the Pond

Written by Sandra Iversen Illustrated by Clive Taylor

A little fish swam up to the side of the pond. "I am hungry," she said. "I want some food."

A big fish swam up to the side of the pond. "I am hungry," she said. "I want some food."

A turtle swam up
to the side of the pond.
"I am hungry," she said.
"I want some food."

A little girl came to the side of the pond.
She had some food.

"Here you are, turtle," said the little girl. "Here is some food for you."

"Thank you," said the turtle, and she swam away.

7

"Here you are, big fish," said the little girl.
"Here is some food for you."

"Thank you," said the big fish, and she swam away.

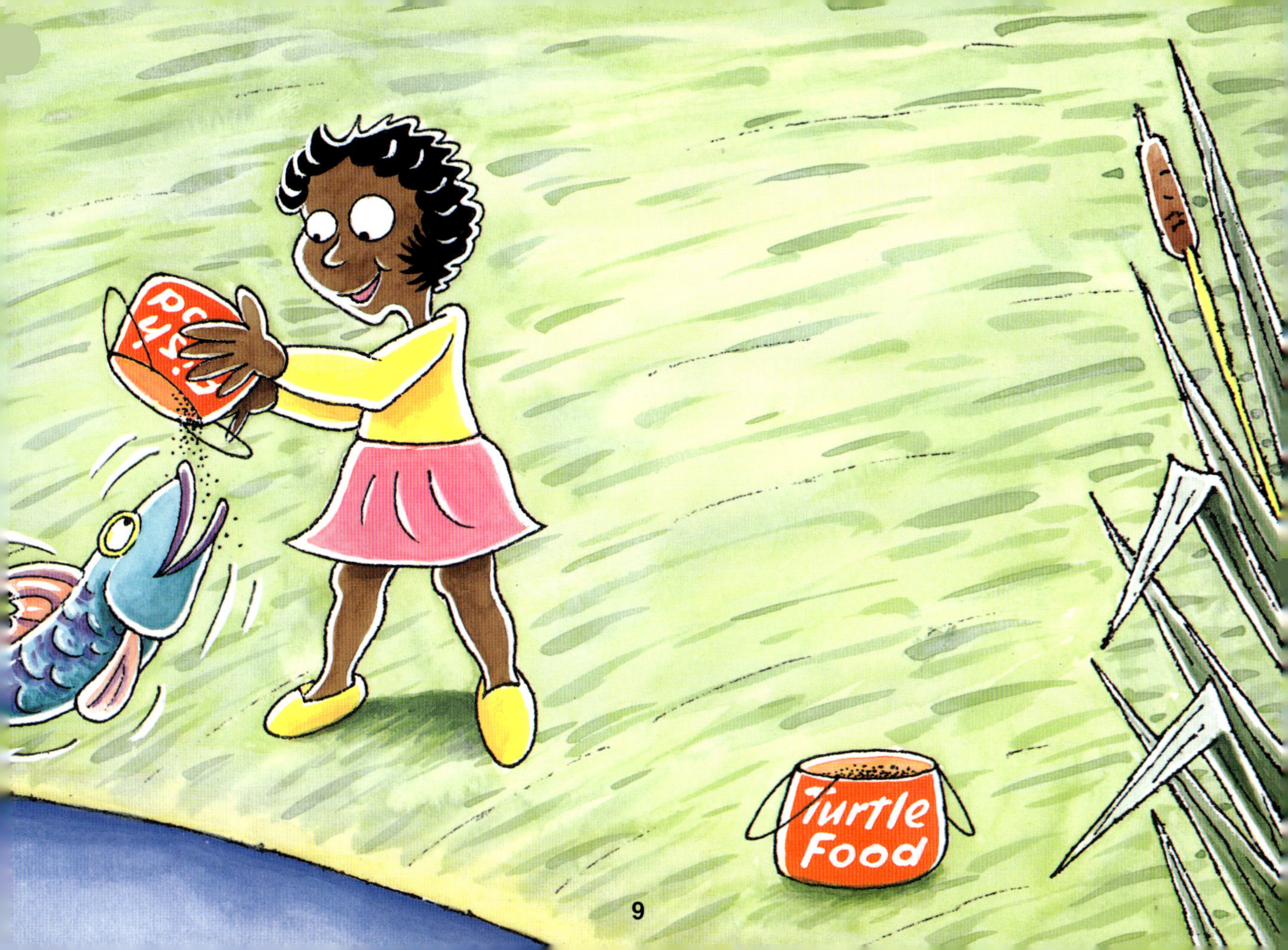
Turtle Food

"Here you are, little fish," said the little girl.
"Here is some food for you."

"Thank you," said the little fish, and she swam away.

11

12